MYTHS & LEGENDS

MYTHS & LEGENDS

PAINTINGS IN THE NATIONAL GALLERY

FELICITY WOOLF

National Gallery Publications
The National Gallery
London

National Gallery Publications
Published by order of the Trustees

British Library Cataloguing in
Publication Data

Woolf, Felicity
National Gallery myths and legends.
1. Mythology in art   2. Legends in
art
I. Title   II. National Gallery
753'.7   ND1420

ISBN 0–947645–08–X

Designed by Laurence Bradbury
Printed and bound in Great Britain
by W. S. Cowell Limited, Ipswich

Cover illustration: Turner, *Ulysses
deriding Polyphemus* (detail)

ACKNOWLEDGEMENTS

Susan Woodford of the London University Extra-Mural department reawakened my enthusiasm for things Greek and Roman, and I would like to thank her most sincerely. At the National Gallery I would like to thank Neil MacGregor, Allan Braham and Christopher Brown, all of whom read the manuscript, and in particular Alistair Smith, who gave me time to work on it and made many helpful suggestions. My editor Lucy Trench has worked tirelessly on the text and rescued the project from extinction on several occasions. Outside the Gallery, Fintan Cullen, Kathleen Adler and Denis Moylan offered advice and encouragement.

It is the public who attend lectures at the National Gallery who made me realise the interest which still exists in classical mythology, and who caused me to read the stories closely and retell them clearly in relation to the paintings, and it is to the public audience that this book is dedicated.

CONTENTS

FOREWORD

The National Gallery represents European Painting from the thirteenth to the early twentieth century, and many of the greatest Western painters are shown at their best in the Collection. Gallery booklets have been devoted in past years to 'Themes and Painters' in the Gallery; volumes on the national schools of painting, illustrated in colour, are in course of publication.

The subject-matter covered by the paintings in the Gallery is exceptionally wide-ranging, and the present book on Myths and Legends is to be the first of a new series of publications devoted, more comprehensively than has been attempted hitherto, to 'themes' in the National Gallery Collection. The author, Felicity Woolf, was until recently a member of the Gallery's Education Department. Her writing about the subject, as the reader will soon discover, is notably enthusiastic, informed and imaginative.

She realised that many of the paintings in the Gallery cover in some detail the subjects of the Trojan War, the wanderings of Odysseus and Aeneas, and especially many of the more celebrated stories from Ovid's *Metamorphoses*, as well as the legends of Venus and Cupid. She shows in the Introduction how closely patrons identified themselves with these subjects and how far they became assimilated into the fabric of Christianity. Understanding more deeply this heritage of myth and knowledge, familiar to painters in earlier centuries, serves – as the following pages make clear – to sharpen our own appreciation of the living artistic achievement of the artists of the past.

ALLAN BRAHAM
KEEPER

INTRODUCTION

Adults and children alike love stories, and the Education Department's daily work in the National Gallery confirms that paintings of myths and legends are especially popular. When these pictures were made the stories illustrated were all well-known and would have required little or no explanation. But now they are often forgotten, and inevitably the visitor loses some enjoyment when he or she cannot quite remember the detail of the narrative. The purpose of this book is primarily to tell the stories illustrated in the pictures, so as to increase the viewer's appreciation and understanding of the artist's interpretation of the narrative.

The paintings date from the fifteenth to the nineteenth century, but they are arranged according to subject-matter rather than when they were made. The first group of paintings illustrates episodes from the legend of the Trojan War, and from the lives of the heroes Ulysses and Aeneas who survived the siege of Troy. The second group is the largest and illustrates stories from Ovid's *Metamorphoses* – a collection of myths of transformation. Until at least the eighteenth century the *Metamorphoses* were more frequently painted than any other text, apart from the Bible. Paintings of the goddess of love, Venus, and her son, Cupid, are the subject of the final section. Most of the paintings in the Gallery based on classical subject-matter fall into these three categories, although inevitably there are some exceptions.

The earliest mythological paintings in the National Gallery were made in Italy in the fifteenth century. Their shapes and sizes often reveal their original location and function, usually as part of household furniture. Like other secular subjects – such as battles and hunting scenes – mythological and legendary subjects first appeared in the home, in tapestries or on panels set into furniture, such as the gilded and painted clothes chests (*cassoni*) sometimes given as part of a bride's dowry (fig. 1). Botticelli's *Venus and Mars* (plate 23) was perhaps part of a bed, while another panel, Piero di Cosimo's *Lapiths and Centaurs* (plate 21), may simply have formed part of the wall-panelling which lined a room instead of more expensive tapestries. It is only at the end of the fifteenth century that paintings of classical subjects become larger, independent of furniture and nearer to our modern idea of an easel painting.

Fig. 1 Fifteenth-century Florentine school. Cassone with a Tournament Scene

The emergence of classical subject-matter in Italian painting in the fifteenth century is part of the artistic and cultural phenomenon known as the Renaissance. In fact, many of the stories illustrated in these Renaissance paintings had been known throughout the Middle Ages and illustrated editions of Ovid's *Metamorphoses* have survived from the fourteenth century. These early book illustrations, however, show the ancient characters, whether mortal or immortal, in contemporary medieval settings and costume. This convention continued throughout the fifteenth century, as can be seen in the National Gallery's *Apollo and Daphne* (plate 8).

As part of the revival of interest in antiquity, during the Renaissance Italian artists began to paint classical subjects in a new way. They approached the material more historically, attempting to show the figures and settings in an authentic, classical manner. Artists studied ancient Roman sculpture, and in their paintings reproduced the costumes, poses and body types that they saw. Fifteenth-century artists realised that Roman sculptors had frequently represented men and gods as nude athletes with idealised bodies, and they adopted this idea of the heroic nude. Similarly, when a classical story required a nymph or goddess to be shown naked, artists looked to surviving statues of Venus for inspiration. This widespread use of the *forms* of ancient art to represent classical stories is what distinguishes Renaissance paintings of classical subjects from earlier illustrations.

Almost no ancient Greek or Roman painting was known in the Renaissance, so the appearance of classical painting could only be imagined with the help of sculpture and written descriptions by writers such as Pliny the Elder (AD 23–79) and Lucian (around AD 117–180). Several National Gallery pictures seem to illustrate these descriptions of

Fig. 2 Albrecht Dürer (1471–1528). Apollo and Diana. *London, British Museum*

lost works (see, for example, plates 18 and 23).

The idea of representing the pagan gods and goddesses *all'antica*, that is in a classical style, originated in Italy and spread only slowly to Northern Europe. From about 1500 in Germany Albrecht Dürer (1471–1528) made prints and drawings of pagan gods, showing the figures with classical proportions (see fig. 2). The first German artist to produce independent panel paintings of mythological subjects was Lucas Cranach the Elder, who worked at the court of the Elector of Saxony in Wittenberg in the early sixteenth century. However, Cranach often reverts to the older tradition and includes figures in contemporary dress, while his female nudes (plate 24) are based on medieval rather than classical models. Two artists from the Netherlands, Jan Gossaert and Martin van Heemskerck, visited Italy at this time and similarly introduced classical forms and subject-matter into their work.

By the end of the sixteenth century artists in certain Northern centres, such as Antwerp and Haarlem, were won over more completely to the principle of painting in the classical style, as can be seen in the *Two Followers of Cadmus* by Cornelis van Haarlem (plate 10). The historian and artist Carel van Mander wrote an enthusiastic account of Cornelis's works in his book about painting, *Het Schilderboeck*, published in 1604. The Cadmus painting is probably the first work referred to in the following passage:

> During the best part of his studies he made an oblong Serpent-biting on a great canvas and another great canvas in a vertical format representing the fall of Lucifer, which two paintings Jacob Rauwart of Amsterdam had from him. Of these two I cannot adequately describe the excellent studies of all the different attitudes of the Nudes and it is a pity that such things cannot be seen in a public place; for at this time he paid a great deal of attention to the art of drawing, of composition, of proportions and other things. (*Het Schilderboeck*, Haarlem [1604], Fol. 293r.).

From this description one might assume that the story behind the Cadmus painting was of little interest to the author. Yet in his book van Mander included a section explaining Ovid's *Metamorphoses* and discussing the meaning of the myths. This paradox brings us to the complicated question of meaning in mythological paintings.

During the Middle Ages scholars attempted to make pagan mythology fit into their Christian system of understanding the world. They did this in various ways. One means of divesting the Olympian gods of their divinity,

Fig. 3 Titian (active before 1511, died 1576). Danaë with Nursemaid. *Madrid, Prado*

yet accepting them as benevolent forces in human existence, was to believe that Jupiter, Saturn, Mercury and the rest had been gifted humans who had been misguidedly raised to the status of the divine by ignorant pagans. The ancient traditions of astrology had assimilated these gods and had given their names to the planets (Venus, Mars etc.), which, even within a Christian universe, exercised influence over human life. Medieval scholars also believed that pagan myths could be interpreted to reveal Christian truths. For example, the chaste nymph Daphne, who rejected Apollo's advances and was turned into a laurel tree (plate 8), was seen as a precursor of the Virgin Mary and representative of the virtue of chastity. Versions of the *Metamorphoses*, known as the *Ovide Moralisé*, which provided this type of Christian commentary, were produced from the fourteenth century first in France and then all over Europe.

The difficulty for modern historians lies in gauging the extent to which these moralising interpretations of the myths should be read into the paintings. Some pictures may simply have been admired for their exciting or romantic stories, which gave artists an opportunity to paint complex compositions, exotic settings and nudes, particularly female ones.

One example of this difficulty is the famous set of mythological paintings or *poesie* (poems) made by Titian for the Spanish king, Philip II, during the 1550s. Although it was never dispatched to Spain, the National Gallery's *Death of Actaeon* (plate 11) was initially intended for this series. Philip was an exceptionally pious man, and Spain was slow to show interest in the new mythological subject-matter of the Italian Renaissance. Scholars have suggested that Philip would have interpreted the paintings as Christian allegories and as instructive moral illustrations of justice and virtue. For example he may have thought of Danaë as a precursor of the Virgin Mary, since Danaë conceived the hero Perseus after she had been penetrated by Jupiter disguised as a shower of gold (fig. 3). Yet Titian's paintings contain some of the most blatantly sensual female nudes ever painted, and it is difficult to set aside the immediate response that the patron enjoyed them as titillating erotica. A letter from Titian to Philip reporting on the progress of the paintings seems to support this less learned interpretation:

> Because the figure of Danaë, which I have already sent to Your Majesty, is seen entirely from the front, I have chosen in this other *poesia* to vary the appearance and show the opposite side, so that the room in which they are to hang will seem more agreeable. Shortly I hope to send you the *poesia* of *Perseus and Andromeda*, which will have a viewpoint different from these two; and likewise *Medea and Jason*. (Quoted by Charles Hope in *Titian*. London 1980, p. 125.)

It is equally difficult to generalise about the meanings of some seventeenth-century paintings with classical subject-matter. Nicolas Poussin and Claude Lorrain both worked in Rome in the middle part of the century. While many of Poussin's paintings of mythological and Stoical subjects were intended for a group of scholarly antiquarians who sought complex meanings in the ancient texts (plate 16), Claude's idealised landscape paintings, based on the scenery around Rome, often included more or less interchangeable classical figures, chosen apparently arbitrarily (for example, the National Gallery's *Landscape with Cephalus and Procris reunited by Diana*).

At the end of his career Claude illustrated several episodes from *The Aeneid*, commissioned by Roman patrons who claimed descent from Aeneas, the legendary founder of Rome. In the *Arrival of Aeneas at Pallanteum*, now at Anglesey Abbey, one of Aeneas' boats bears the coat of arms of the patron's adopted family, the Altieri. If Titian's or Botticelli's patrons liked to think they were looking at a recreation of a lost classical

Fig. 4 Giovanni Battista Tiepolo (1696–1770). An Allegory
with Venus and Time

painting, some of Claude's patrons must have felt they were asserting their
personal connection with a Roman landscape once peopled with legendary
heroes.

Such personal, dynastic statements continue to be made during the
eighteenth century. The *Allegory with Venus and Time* by G. B. Tiepolo in the
National Gallery (fig. 4) formed the central part of a ceiling decoration in a
private Venetian palace. The baby passed to Time by Venus is probably a
portrait of a child of the Contarini family who commissioned the painting.
Here the suggestion may be that the child is Aeneas, who was believed to be

the son of Venus. Venetian Rococo paintings such as this often rework sixteenth-century compositions, substituting private meanings for public. Many of the earlier mythological and allegorical paintings had been set into the ceilings of public rooms in civic buildings to glorify the Venetian state, but Tiepolo's ceiling canvas glorifies a single family.

Classical subject-matter remained standard source material for Romantic artists in the nineteenth century. Sometimes these artists chose myths or legends which they felt reflected their own experiences and emotions. *Ovid among the Scythians* (fig. 5), which shows the poet Ovid exiled from Rome among barbarians, may express Delacroix's own feelings of rejection and isolation. In *Ulysses deriding Polyphemus* (plate 6) Turner was probably using myth to represent both recent scientific discoveries and his perception of the strength of natural forces such as the sun. However, John Ruskin, a great supporter of Turner, suggested that the artist chose the subject of Ulysses escaping from the Cyclops in order to express the idea of his own enlightenment in contrast to blind and ignorant public taste:

> He had been himself shut up by one-eyed people, in a cave 'darkened with laurels' . . . he had seen his companions eaten in the cave by the one-eyed people – (many a painter of good promise had fallen by

Fig. 5 Ferdinand-Victor-Eugène Delacroix (1798–1863). Ovid among the Scythians

Fig. 6 Pablo Picasso (1881–1973). Centaur, Bacchant and Faun *London, Victoria and Albert Museum*

Turner's side in those early toils of his); at last, when his own time had like to have come, he thrust the rugged pine-trunk – all ablaze – . . . into the faces of the one-eyed people, left them tearing their hair in the cloud-banks – got out of the cave in a humble way, under a sheep's belly . . . and got away to open sea as the dawn broke over the Enchanted Islands. (*The Works of John Ruskin*, ed. E. T. Cook and A. Wedderburn, London 1904, Vol. XIII pp. 136–7).

At the end of the nineteenth century, the convention of using classical forms for figures, established since the Renaissance, began to be challenged. However, classical myth and legend have continued to play an important part in twentieth-century art, as can be seen particularly in Picasso's graphic work, where minotaurs, centaurs, satyrs and fauns form part of a witty and suggestive vocabulary (fig. 6).

THE TROJAN WAR

Ancient Greek literature tells of a war between the Greeks and the Trojans, caused because Paris, a Trojan prince, had abducted Helen, queen of Sparta, and taken her back to Troy. It was said that a Greek force sailed east to Troy to recover Helen, and that the Greeks besieged Troy for ten years before they finally destroyed the city. In the late nineteenth century a prehistoric site was excavated in Turkey, on the east coast of the Aegean at the entrance to the Dardanelles, a position which accords with the literary descriptions of Troy. Several strata of building were revealed, including a Mycenaean settlement, and some scholars believe that this was the city of Troy besieged by the Greeks.

For centuries, legends about the Trojan War were passed on by spoken tradition. Some of these were gathered together, perhaps in the eighth century BC, in *The Iliad*. This, the most famous poem about the war, describes the events of a few days in the ten-year siege, concentrating on the quarrel between two of the Greek leaders, Agamemnon and Achilles. The author of the poem is said to be Homer, although there is considerable debate about when and where he lived, and when the poem was written down. Greek and Roman writers also took up the biographies of particular heroes after the fall of Troy. *The Aeneid*, a Latin epic written by Virgil in the first century BC, tells the story of Aeneas, a Trojan prince who escaped from the burning city, while the long voyage home of the Greek hero Odysseus (Latin form, Ulysses) is recounted in *The Odyssey*, also believed to be by Homer.

Some of the most frequently painted episodes connected with the Trojan War, such as the Judgement of Paris or the Abduction of Helen, are not in Homer but were recounted in other Greek poems. These poems are now lost, but they were an important source for writers of later antiquity, whose poems in their turn inspired medieval poets. Medieval romances based on the legends of the Trojan War were written in Europe from the late thirteenth century onwards. They were immensely popular and ensured that the stories of the siege were well known and frequently used by Western painters.

The paintings that follow show episodes before and during the siege of Troy, and also the adventures of Odysseus and Aeneas. They date from the fifteenth to the nineteenth century.

10

THE JUDGEMENT OF PARIS

According to legend, the Trojan War was caused by envy and rivalry among the Olympian gods and goddesses. The trouble began at the wedding feast of Peleus and Thetis, to which all the Immortals had been invited except Eris, goddess of discord. Eris decided to provoke a quarrel and threw down a golden apple inscribed 'To the fairest'. Three goddesses, Juno, Minerva and Venus, considered themselves to be the rightful winner of the prize. To resolve the argument Mercury, messenger of the gods, took the goddesses to Mount Ida and displayed them to a shepherd.

The shepherd's name was Paris, and he was also the son of Priam, king of Troy. He had been abandoned at birth because his mother Hecuba had dreamt that she would give birth to a fiery torch issuing snakes. This dream was felt to be so bad an omen that Hecuba was advised to abandon her offspring. As it happened, the baby was rescued and cared for by shepherds on Mount Ida.

Mercury told Paris to award the golden apple to whomever he considered to be the most beautiful. The three goddesses tried to bribe Paris: Minerva, goddess of strength and wisdom, guaranteed him glory in war; Juno, queen of the gods, offered him Asia and great wealth; Venus, goddess of love, promised him possession of Helen, the most beautiful woman in the world. Paris chose beauty and love, and gave the golden apple to Venus.

The Judgement of Paris had been illustrated throughout the Middle Ages, but had particular appeal in the Renaissance because it gave artists an opportunity to depict idealised female nudes from three viewpoints. The subject offered the patron both aesthetic and erotic pleasure, while the women's mythological 'disguise' ensured a certain decorum. It was frequently painted in the Netherlands around 1600, and the National Gallery's small-scale version of the subject (plate 1), executed in Utrecht by Joachim Wtewael, is dated 1615.

The Immortals' banquet is shown in the background and Eris hovers above the table where the gods and goddesses are celebrating. Various traditional attributes identify the characters in the judgement scene in the foreground. Mercury wears a winged hat and holds a caduceus, a magic wand carried by messengers and sometimes associated with healing. Venus is shown with her winged son Cupid, who playfully threatens Paris with his bow – people who are struck by Cupid's arrows are destined to fall in love. The two other goddesses stand ignored. Minerva, on the right, can be identified by her helmet and shield and the owl hovering above Mercury,

1. Joachim Wtewael (1566–1638). The Judgement of Paris

while the peacock sitting in the tree in the top left belongs to Juno.

Wtewael has emphasised the erotic potential of the subject: the figures are in complex twisting and interlocking poses, and the colours are hot and saturated, with strong contrasts. The goat was traditionally considered to be lascivious, while the exotic shells suggest female pudenda.

This painting also reflects the long tradition in Northern European painting of depicting flowers and other natural phenomena in precise detail. The botanical exactitude suggests comparison with the new genre of still-life painting, which was developing at this time in the Netherlands.

The second *Judgement of Paris* illustrated here (plate 2) was painted by Rubens around 1635, about twenty years after Wtewael's rendering. As in the earlier picture, the three goddesses are clearly identified by their attributes: Minerva by her armour; Venus by Cupid; and Juno by a peacock. But the moment of judgement is presented with more tension and uncertainty. Both Juno and Venus turn towards Paris. Does Venus' gesture suggest she realises she is the winner?

In a less crowded, pastoral landscape, Rubens evokes Paris' life as a shepherd. Sheep graze beneath the trees and the dog glares at the hissing peacock. The idyllic nature of this scene, however, belies the outcome of the competition; Rubens points to the ensuing tragedy by depicting Alecto, one of the three Furies or spirits of vengeance, hovering in the sky above.

Rubens was extremely well-read in classical literature. In addition to the traditional sources, he may well have been aware of a passage in a *Dialogue* by the Greek writer Lucian (second century AD), which tells how Paris asked the goddesses to undress to allow him to judge fairly. X-radiographs of the panel have revealed that his initial idea was to paint the goddesses in

2. Peter Paul Rubens (1577–1640). The Judgement of Paris

the act of disrobing. Cupid was at first to be painted beside Venus, helping her take off her cloak.

Rubens painted the Judgement of Paris several times and there are two versions by him in the National Gallery; this is the later one, painted in the last decade of his life. The artist's mature technique demonstrates his brilliance as a draughtsman and as a colourist. He was able to depict the particular quality of any material and this work is remarkable for the range of textures represented – feathers, skin, fur, metal, leaves, and so on. As a result the sensuality of the subject is fully realised. The fleshy nudes present three views of the female form; pale bodies are set against dark foils. The spectator is teased – Venus' full beauty is revealed only to Paris.

THE ABDUCTION OF HELEN

Paris sailed to Sparta to claim Helen, the reward that Venus had promised him. According to the popular medieval romances which made this episode well-known, Helen left willingly with Paris. Medieval French and Italian poets described how Paris saw her worshipping with friends and attendants in the temple of Apollo and Diana on the island of Cythera. When they met, Helen, though married to Menelaus, king of Sparta, fell in love with Paris and eloped with him to Troy.

A small panel (plate 3), probably painted around 1450 in Florence by a follower of Fra Angelico, illustrates a medieval interpretation of the story. The temple of Apollo and Diana is on the right, while Paris' waiting ship is in the background on the left. The spear-shaped tree in the centre leads the eye to Paris, carrying Helen on his back; other women are being carried off by Paris' companions. The small child in the centre foreground may be Cupid, Venus' son, whose arrows caused Paris and Helen to fall in love.

The painter has interpreted the story in contemporary terms, and most of the figures wear the elaborate and costly dress of wealthy mid-fifteenth-century Florentines. The armour of the soldiers on the left is perhaps meant to suggest classical armour, but other men wear the hose and short tunic favoured by young noblemen when they went riding. Helen wears a silk gown with attached fur-lined sleeves.

The panel is in good condition, which suggests that it was never set into furniture – panels removed from chests or other types of furniture tend to be damaged. There are surviving examples of painted trays given to

3. Follower of Fra Angelico (active 1417, died 1455). The Abduction of Helen

celebrate a marriage or the birth of a child. The *Abduction of Helen* was not a tray, but may relate to that custom; it is possible that this romantic representation of the legend was a betrothal gift.

THE SIEGE OF TROY

In an attempt to reclaim Helen, a Greek force led by Menelaus and his brother Agamemnon sailed to Troy. They besieged the city for ten years but only achieved their final victory by means of a trick. The Greeks built a huge wooden horse and wrote a dedicatory inscription on its flank to the goddess Minerva, known in Greek as Pallas Athene. Hiding some of their warriors inside, they then left the horse outside the walls of Troy and pretended to sail home.

Relieved by the Greeks' departure, the Trojans came to look at the mysterious apparition, but were undecided as to how to react. The priest

Laocoön was convinced that the horse would bring disaster to the city, and he hurled his spear into its flank to show that it was hollow. But Sinon, a spy planted by the Greeks, persuaded the Trojans that Athene would be offended if they left the horse outside the gates. Later, two huge snakes suddenly appeared from the sea and devoured Laocoön and his sons. The Trojans could no longer doubt Sinon, and they dragged the horse up to the citadel.

That night the Greeks crept out of the horse, opened the city gates to the main part of their forces, who were hiding nearby, and stormed the citadel. The Trojans were defeated, and the Greeks took their revenge for Paris' abduction of Helen.

Two paintings (plates 4 and 5) in the National Gallery illustrate the episode of the wooden horse. They were executed around the middle of the eighteenth century by Giovanni Domenico Tiepolo, who worked in a style close to that of his more famous father, Giovanni Battista Tiepolo. The silhouetting of forms against the sky and the extreme contrast in scale between the figures in the foreground and background are typical of the

4. Giovanni Domenico Tiepolo (1727–1804). The Building of the Trojan Horse

5. Giovanni Domenico Tiepolo (1727–1804). The Procession of the Trojan Horse into Troy

dramatic effects favoured by the Tiepolo family. Both pictures are probably sketches for a series of larger paintings illustrating scenes of the fall of Troy. Only one larger composition still exists, possibly related to the *Building of the Trojan Horse* sketch.

Both sketches show that Tiepolo had detailed knowledge of the story of the fall of Troy, as told by Virgil in *The Aeneid* and by other classical authors. Virgil tells how Cassandra, Priam's daughter, was arrested after she, like Laocoön, prophesied disaster if the horse were brought into the city; this incident can be made out in the background of the *Procession of the Trojan Horse into Troy* (plate 5). It is less easy to identify the background figures in the *Building of the Trojan Horse* (plate 4). The man pointing could be Odysseus, who played an important part in devising the horse, or Agamemnon, while the man behind him could be Sinon, the spy, or possibly Odysseus.

THE RETURN OF ULYSSES

After the fall of Troy, Ulysses, one of the Greek heroes, began his ten-year journey home to Ithaca. He was known to the Greeks as Odysseus, and Homer's *Odyssey* tells how he was subjected to a series of dangerous adventures, including capture by the one-eyed giant Polyphemus. Ulysses was trapped in Polyphemus' cave with twelve companions, whom the giant began to eat two by two. It was Ulysses' legendary cunning which defeated the giant. The Greek made the giant drunk and drowsy with magic wine, then pierced his single eye with a sharp stick. Ulysses and his remaining men escaped from the cave by concealing themselves in the fleeces of the blinded giant's sheep as they went out to graze. They rejoined the waiting crew on board ship and set sail, although Ulysses could not resist taunting the giant, who threw a huge rock at their departing boat.

6. Joseph Mallord William Turner (1775–1851). Ulysses deriding Polyphemus

In Turner's interpretation of the scene (plate 6) the giant is seated clutching his head on the mountain top. Though indistinct in the vaporous atmosphere, he can be seen on the left of the painting. Nereids, or sea nymphs, swim in front of the boat as it speeds away. Their transparent forms represent the phenomenon of phosphorescence in the water. On a flag in the rigging is a picture of the Trojan horse, reminding us that Ulysses played a part in the invention of the treacherous beast. Other ships in Ulysses' fleet are silhouetted against the sun on the right.

The main subject of the painting, however, seems to be the explosion of dawn light as the sun rises from the sea. The light appears as a celebration of Ulysses' escape from the darkness of the giant's cave, represented on the left side of the painting. Horses — probably inspired by the pedimental sculptures from the Parthenon — rear from the sea to carry the sun on its journey across the sky. This is a painting rich in every type of reference to classical antiquity: literary, visual and symbolic.

When the picture was exhibited at the Royal Academy in 1829 some critics remarked on the spectacular, vibrant colouring, with its high key, abundance of white and yellow, and lack of conventional black shadows. It is one of the first large-scale oil paintings in which Turner used the palette that later became characteristic of his representations of light.

For Ruskin, Turner's great champion, this was 'to be considered as the *central picture* in Turner's career'. He suggested that the painting had a particularly personal significance (see pages 8–9) and said the sky was 'beyond comparison the finest that exists in Turner's oil-paintings'.

AENEAS TAKES REFUGE ON DELOS

Aeneas, a Trojan prince, escaped from the fallen city with his father, Anchises, and his son Ascanius. They took refuge on the island of Delos where an important temple was dedicated to Apollo. Aeneas and his father were greeted by the white-robed King Anius, a priest of Apollo, who showed them two famous trees, a palm and an olive, where Apollo and his twin sister Diana had been born. The immortal twins had been conceived from an illicit union between Latona and Jupiter, and the island of Delos was the only place which agreed to shelter Latona while she was giving birth. In thanks she promised that her son, Apollo, would establish his temple on the island.

7. *Claude (1600–1682).* Landscape with Aeneas at Delos

Claude Gellée, called Le Lorrain, after his birthplace, settled in Rome in the early 1620s and specialised in paintings of landscapes and seaports (see plates 12 and 26). He made open-air sketches of the scenery, buildings and vegetation in and around Rome, studying them at different times of the day. These drawings were the basis of his credible but idealised landscape fantasies, in which the 'scenery' is arranged like 'flats' on a stage set. Lighting effects play over delicate, airy trees, architectural ruins and reconstructed classical buildings. The domed temple in plate 7 for example is a fanciful version of the ancient Roman Pantheon.

Sometimes Claude's figures seem extraneous to their settings, but his imaginative recreation of the island of Delos (plate 7) is one of his finest mature works, with a complete integration of figure-subject and setting. The literary sources told how the travellers were shown the temple of Apollo and entertained by the priest-king Anius in his house, the portico of which is visible on the extreme right. Aeneas' journey and the island setting justify the seascape; even the trees are accounted for as those of Apollo's birthplace.

The most obvious text to which one would expect Claude to have referred is Virgil's *Aeneid*. This tells the story of Aeneas' wanderings, his landing on the Italian peninsula and his role in the foundation of Rome. There is no doubt that in five other paintings executed during the last ten years of his life, Claude illustrated episodes as they are told in *The Aeneid*. However, in this painting of 1672, the first in Claude's work to show Aeneas, it seems that the artist was visualising a passage in Book XIII of Ovid's poem, *Metamorphoses*.

Metamorphoses, as we shall see, is a collection of classical myths about transformation; the Trojan War and its aftermath are only described incidentally. But Ovid writes of Aeneas' escape from Troy, the journey to Delos, Anius' greeting and the two sacred trees – and the latter detail is not included by Virgil. It seems likely that the Ovidian passage first aroused Claude's interest in the story of Aeneas and perhaps inspired him to read or re-read *The Aeneid* itself.

OVID'S 'METAMORPHOSES'

The poem *Metamorphoses* was written by Ovid, a Roman poet, in the first few years of the first century AD and contains about two hundred and fifty stories of transformation. These explain how many natural phenomena – animals, trees, plants, rivers – were originally mortals or divinities who had been changed into a new form. Ovid rarely invented the stories: the poem is a compilation of various Greek myths popular in early imperial Rome. Its novelty is in the gathering together of the material and the entertaining and descriptive narrative.

Ovid himself incurred the wrath of the Emperor Augustus and in 8AD was banished to a bleak fishing village on the shores of the Black Sea. His petitions for mercy failed and he spent the last ten years of his life among primitive tribes. Ovid's exile is the subject of a painting in the National Gallery by Delacroix (fig. 5).

During the Italian Renaissance, when a taste developed for large-scale secular paintings with figures in the classical style, it was the myths from *Metamorphoses* that were most frequently illustrated. Gradually the taste for such secular paintings spread all over Europe, and the National Gallery holds *Metamorphoses* paintings from several European centres, dating from the fifteenth to the eighteenth century. Their sequence in this section follows that of the stories in the poem.

APOLLO AND DAPHNE

Apollo considered himself invincible after he had killed the serpent Python and in his triumph he mocked Cupid's puny weapons. In revenge, Cupid wounded Apollo with one of his sharpest arrows, making him fall in love with the nymph Daphne, daughter of the river god Peneus. But Cupid had fired a lead-tipped arrow at Daphne, so that she would never fall in love. Although Apollo was captivated by her beauty Daphne rejected his advances. Finally, inflamed with desire, Apollo tried to force himself on Daphne and gave chase as she fled through the woods.

8. Ascribed to Antonio del Pollaiuolo (c.1432–1498) Apollo and Daphne

The god was almost touching her when Daphne saw the river Peneus and cried out to her father to save her. Ovid writes:

> Her prayer was scarcely ended when a deep languor took hold on her limbs, her soft breast was enclosed in thin bark, her hair grew into leaves, her arms into branches, and her feet that were lately so swift were held fast by sluggish roots, while her face became a treetop. (*Metamorphoses*, Book I, p. 43.)

Apollo declared that the tree should be the evergreen laurel and that he would always wear a wreath of laurel leaves, which would never fade.

The story is illustrated in a panel (plate 8) probably painted by one of the Pollaiuolo brothers, either Antonio or Piero, who worked as painters and sculptors in Florence in the second half of the fifteenth century. Although the story follows Ovid's text faithfully, the artist has represented the characters in contemporary Florentine dress, and the valley of the river Peneus winding away into the background is probably a view of the Arno valley outside Florence. Like other Florentine artists, Antonio and Piero Pollaiuolo often included this local view as the background in their paintings; it can, for instance, be seen in their *Martyrdom of Saint Sebastian* in the National Gallery. The representation of aerial perspective, with the colours tending to become indistinct and bluish in the distance, was probably learned from studying imported Netherlandish paintings.

Antonio Pollaiuolo was well known during his lifetime for his rendering of the male figure, especially in movement. He painted the first large-scale representations of the Labours of Hercules to be seen in Florence. They are lost now, but hung in the Medici palace, perhaps as early as the 1460s. From its small size and shape, it seems likely that *Apollo and Daphne* was the door of a small cabinet or the lid of a box, perhaps for jewellery.

JUPITER AND IO

The illicit loves of Jupiter, king of the gods, are a recurring theme in Ovid's poem. On one occasion Jupiter fell in love with the beautiful nymph Io, daughter of the river god Inachus. Like Daphne, Io ran away from her would-be lover, but as soon as she had left behind her familiar surroundings (suggested by the tiny, distant landscape in the bottom left of Lastman's picture, plate 9), the god darkened the earth with clouds and seduced her.

9. Pieter Lastman (1583–1633). Juno discovering Jupiter with Io

Juno, Jupiter's wife, was constantly on the alert for evidence of her husband's infidelities and her suspicions were aroused by the unnatural darkness on earth. She came down from Olympus to investigate and found Jupiter with his arms around a beautiful cow – the god had transformed the unfortunate nymph to disguise his infidelity. Juno insisted on being given the cow as a present and Jupiter could not refuse.

Juno asked Argus, who had a hundred eyes, some of which were always open, to guard the valuable animal. But Jupiter loved Io so much that he sent Mercury to lull Argus to sleep by playing the pipes and telling stories. Once Argus was asleep Mercury cut off his head, and the hundred eyes were taken by Juno to be set in the tail of her bird, the peacock. In the painting, the 'eyes' of the peacock's tail are a dull colour, to give the impression that they have not yet received Argus' eyes. Finally Jupiter begged Juno's forgiveness and Io was changed back into a nymph.

Although no one else is present in Ovid's narrative, Lastman has taken the concept of deceit, the essential ingredient of Jupiter's behaviour, and represented it as a man wearing a fox-pelt and mask, both symbols of falsehood. The irony implicit in the situation also seems to have interested the artist. First, there is dramatic irony in the fact that Jupiter and the viewer know of the deception, while Juno remains literally and metaphorically in the dark, represented by the clouds on the left side of the painting. Then there is perhaps a visual irony in the representation of Jupiter. He is shown nude, with a heroic, muscular body which in Italian painting is a convention implying virtue and strength. But in this situation his nude torso adjacent to the large head of the cow, and his guilty expression, contrive to make him appear ridiculous.

Pieter Lastman worked in Amsterdam from about 1605 to his death in 1633; this work is signed and dated 1618. He was one of a group of Dutch artists who painted mythological and religious narratives, concentrating particularly on realistic settings and the dramatic potential of the stories. Lastman frequently chose subjects where the protagonist has to make a significant moral decision. Rembrandt was briefly a pupil of Lastman in 1623, and many of his early paintings are based on Lastman's designs.

THE STORY OF CADMUS

In Book III of *Metamorphoses*, Cadmus, founder of the city of Thebes, is associated with violent deaths. He unwittingly caused some of his followers to be devoured by a monstrous serpent; his grandson, Actaeon, was torn to death by his own hounds; and his daughter, Semele, burned to ashes at the sight of Jupiter. The first of these episodes is illustrated in the National Gallery in a painting by Cornelis van Haarlem (plate 10).

King Agenor sent his son Cadmus to look for his daughter Europa, who was another victim of Jupiter's amorous attentions. Exiled from his native land until he found his sister, Cadmus finally visited Apollo's oracle for guidance. The oracle instructed him to follow a heifer until she lay down in empty pasture land, and there to found a new city, Thebes. Everything happened as the oracle foretold, until Cadmus' attendants went to fetch water to make an offering to Jupiter. The spring was inside a cave, the home of the fierce snake of Mars, which attacked Cadmus' men and killed them. After a terrible fight, Cadmus succeeded in destroying the snake. He then sowed the serpent's teeth in the ground and from them emerged warriors who helped him to found Thebes. The grotesque spectacle of the

10. Cornelis van Haarlem (1562–1638). Two Followers of Cadmus devoured by a Dragon

dragon-like serpent devouring two men fills the foreground of the painting, while in the left background can be seen the sequel, in which Cadmus kills the monster.

Cornelis worked in Haarlem from about 1583 until his death in 1638, as part of a particularly gifted group of artists who were gathered in the city. Some of them produced new types of naturalistic landscape paintings and prints, while others concentrated on large-scale figure paintings, often with mythological subjects. Cornelis was probably influenced and encouraged by his friend Carel van Mander, the author of a book on painting whose comments on this picture can be found in the Introduction (page 4). Van Mander wanted Dutch artists to rival the great Italian masters in the subjects they depicted and the style they adopted. In this picture the classical subject-matter, the painterly technique, with its broad, free brush-strokes, and the heroic figures are all Italianate, and suggest van Mander's influence. Also, with Cornelis and Hendrick Goltzius, van Mander founded an academy in Haarlem for the study of the live model. This painting, which is dated 1588, is a kind of virtuoso performance showing the artist's mastery of anatomy and composition. That same year a print of the painting was made by Goltzius, who was also a skilled engraver, in order to make the design more widely known.

THE DEATH OF ACTAEON

The next story told by Ovid is of the death of Actaeon, Cadmus' grandson; it is illustrated in the National Gallery in a painting by Titian (plate 11). Actaeon had been out hunting with his companions until the heat of the sun forced them to rest. Wandering in the shady woods, he accidentally surprised Diana, the virgin huntress, bathing with her nymphs. Angry at her exposure to the eyes of a mortal and wishing to prevent anyone from hearing of her humiliation, the goddess splashed water on Actaeon's head. Antlers sprouted where the drops fell and quickly Actaeon was metamorphosed into a stag. He tried to run away, but his own hounds caught his scent and gave chase. Actaeon's friends called to him that they had found a new quarry, but in his bestial state Actaeon could not cry out for help as the dogs tore him to pieces.

The story is particularly cruel and Ovid declares that Diana's punishment was arbitrary and unjustified. Titian's painting seems to emphasise the tragic irony; Actaeon's companions can be seen on horseback in the depths of the wood, to the right of Diana's bow, and Actaeon is still partly human as he is brought down by the dogs. However, during the Renaissance the story was understood as an example of justice: Actaeon's 'violation' of Diana, who personified chastity, upset the natural order, which was restored by his death. This moralising interpretation may explain the presence of Diana, who in Ovid's account does not witness Actaeon's death.

A narrow range of predominantly dark, earth colours have been used – brown, black, yellow and orange – and it seems reasonable to suggest that the sombre landscape is intended to echo the tragedy and brutality of the action. It is possible, though, that this effect is emphasised more than Titian intended. The paint surface has almost certainly darkened with age, and also the picture may be unfinished. The *Death of Actaeon* was found in

11. Titian (active before 1511, died 1576). The Death of Actaeon

Titian's studio at his death in 1576, and a description by a pupil of his late painting technique suggests that Titian began by laying in the design in dark colours and only added lighter colours in the final stages, which in this case he may never have reached.

Titian's dramatic, sensual, and highly original interpretations of the stories from *Metamorphoses* were celebrated in his lifetime. In the 1550s he supplied the Spanish king, Philip II, with a series of these mythologies, or *poesie* (poems) as they were called, and was asked to repeat some of the designs for the Emperor Maximilian, ruler of another Habsburg court in Vienna. The *Death of Actaeon* is mentioned in a letter of 1559 from Titian to Philip II, but for an unknown reason it was never dispatched.

The earlier *poesie*, such as *Bacchus and Ariadne* (plate 18), seem to have been illustrations of scholarly programmes, provided for the artist by the patron and relating to classical descriptions of ancient works of art. But the later mythological paintings – as we saw in the Introduction – were probably intended as sophisticated erotica, and to show off Titian's particular skills as an artist. They placed painting on a level with poetry, and proclaimed the supremacy of Venetian painting, with its reliance on colour as opposed to drawing, for the illustration of classical narrative.

NARCISSUS AND ECHO

T he stories of Narcissus and Echo are less those of transformation than of tragic disembodiment. Echo was punished by Juno for keeping her talking while her husband Jupiter was making love to various nymphs; this gave them time to run away before Juno arrived. After her punishment Echo could only repeat the last words she heard spoken and could never

12. Claude (1600–1682). Landscape with Narcissus and Echo

13. Follower of Giovanni Antonio Boltraffio (c. 1467–1516). Narcissus

begin a conversation herself. When she fell in love with the beautiful Narcissus she was unable to win his affection and pined away until only her voice was left.

Narcissus cruelly rejected Echo, and in retaliation a spirit of the woods decreed that he should fall in love with his own reflection. Narcissus then gazed at himself in a clear, woodland pool until he wasted away. When the nymphs searched for his body it could not be found and instead of his corpse they found the narcissus flower. Ovid tells us that even after death Narcissus kept looking at himself in the Styx, the river of the underworld.

Two paintings in the National Gallery illustrate this story. One, painted in 1644, is by Claude (plate 12), who was primarily a landscape painter and selected subjects which required a landscape setting. This seems to illustrate Ovid's description of the fatal pool that attracted Narcissus:

> There was a clear pool, with shining silvery waters, where shepherds had never made their way; no goats that pasture on the mountains, no cattle had ever come there. Its peace was undisturbed by bird or beast

or falling branches. Around it was a grassy sward, kept ever green by the nearby waters; encircling woods sheltered the spot from the fierce sun, and made it always cool. (*Metamorphoses*, Book III, p. 85).

In Claude's painting the nymph Echo lies sleeping beside the woodland pool and Narcissus is a tiny figure in an extensive landscape. Hidden in the trees are the wood nymphs who later mourned Narcissus.

The other painting (plate 13) is by an unknown follower of Boltraffio, who appears to have been Leonardo's principal pupil in Milan; it was possibly executed around 1510. The artist has concentrated on the essence of the story – Narcissus' self-obsession. The pure profile is bent over a basin of water and the head dominates the picture surface – a composition that suggests total introspection. The image probably derives from drawings that Leonardo passed on to his followers in Milan, where he worked in the 1480s and 1490s. There are some drawings by Leonardo of heads of indeterminate sex, with long curly hair decorated with a wreath of leaves. Ovid's description of Narcissus, whose beauty attracted both male and female admirers, seems to have inspired Leonardo and his followers to explore this androgynous, idealised type.

PERSEUS AND ANDROMEDA

Perseus is one of the heroes of *Metamorphoses*. He was half-man and half-god since he had been conceived when Jupiter, disguised as a shower of gold, seduced the mortal Danaë. One of Perseus' first exploits was to decapitate Medusa, the Gorgon whose fearful head and hair of serpents turned any onlooker to stone. Perseus avoided this fate himself by looking only at a reflection of her in his shield. On his way home he came across Andromeda chained to a rock as a sacrifice to a sea monster. Having first ensured that he would be given her hand in marriage, Perseus attacked the monster, escaping from its snapping jaws with the help of his magical winged sandals, and delivering a mortal blow with his hooked sword.

Andromeda was duly married to Perseus, and the wedding was followed by a great banquet. Just as Perseus was telling how he had cut off the Gorgon's head, the festivities were interrupted – Phineas had come to claim Andromeda, for she had been promised to him before Perseus' arrival.

This huge canvas by Luca Giordano (plate 14) illustrates the ensuing fight, described in great detail by Ovid. Perseus has been outnumbered and as a last resort has taken out the Gorgon's head. Phineas, in yellow, and his two companions are turning to stone, from the head and fingertips down, as they hurl their spears at Perseus. From a mass of detailed description and minor incident Giordano has created an intense moment of confrontation. The Gorgon's head is the compelling central focus of his composition: bodies litter the floor, tables topple, people flee in terror, but one's eye always returns to the writhing snakes and gaping mouth of Medusa.

Perseus was probably commissioned in the 1680s for an important public room in a Genoese palace. Over fourteen feet wide, it is the largest

14. Luca Giordano (1634–1705). Perseus turning Phineas and his Followers to Stone

mythological painting in the National Gallery, very different in its purpose and effect from the small-scale, cabinet pieces such as Wtewael's *Judgement of Paris* (plate 1) or Lastman's *Juno discovering Jupiter and Io* (plate 9), which were to be handled and admired at close quarters.

Luca Giordano was Neapolitan, but worked all over Italy and also in Spain. He was admired for his speed of execution and the grandeur of his designs. This work derives ultimately from sixteenth-century Venetian paintings, which featured elaborate architectural backgrounds and splendid banqueting scenes. The macabre subject, with its profusion of dead bodies and the severed head, probably reflects Neapolitan taste. The frozen group of three warriors on the left is perhaps based on Giordano's study of the *Borghese Warrior*, a classical sculpture of a man throwing a weapon. This allusion to a famous sculpture is possibly intended to draw attention to Giordano's technical virtuosity in showing human flesh in the process of turning to stone.

The battle appears to be taking place on a stage – the proscenium arch is suggested by the curtain on the right and by dark 'flats' on both sides. Strong rays of light stream in from the top left. In striving to represent the spectacular, seventeenth-century Italian artists frequently adapted conventions and devices used in the theatre.

THE STORY OF CEPHALUS

In Book VII of *Metamorphoses* Cephalus tells his own poignant story, one of mistrust and misunderstanding. Cephalus was married to Procris, a beautiful Athenian woman. They lived together happily until Aurora, goddess of the dawn, became attracted to Cephalus and tried to seduce him away from his wife when he was out hunting. Although Cephalus remained faithful and Aurora was forced to release him, she cursed his love for Procris. Returning home, Cephalus grew suspicious of Procris and decided to test her fidelity. He disguised himself and made advances to Procris, promising her a fortune in return for one night alone with her. At first Procris refused, but, much to Cephalus' distress, eventually she weakened. When Cephalus revealed his true identity Procris fled in shame to live in the woods with the nymphs of the virgin huntress, Diana.

It was only when Cephalus had begged his wife's forgiveness that Diana reunited the lovers. Procris returned with two gifts from Diana, a dog which

15. Peter Paul Rubens (1577–1640). Aurora abducting Cephalus

could run faster than any other and a javelin which never missed its mark. The couple then shared some years together before a final tragedy ensued.

Taking the javelin, Cephalus went out hunting every morning and could be heard inviting the cool breeze, Zephyr, to refresh him. Someone unfortunately mistook this 'Zephyr' for a nymph and told Procris that her husband was being unfaithful. The next day she rushed from home distraught and hid near Cephalus when he rested after hunting. He heard a rustling sound in the undergrowth and threw his javelin, fatally wounding his own wife. As Procris died in his arms, he could only assure her that Zephyr was not his mistress.

The painting by Rubens (plate 15) illustrates Aurora's meeting with Cephalus – she steps from her chariot to embrace the reluctant hunter as his dogs lie nearby. Painted around 1636 or 1637, it is a sketch made to serve as a model for a larger, finished painting, one of a series commissioned by Philip IV to decorate a hunting lodge, the Torre de la Parada near Madrid.

Nicolas Poussin, in a painting probably executed around 1630 (plate 16), shows Cephalus resisting Aurora and turning to look at a portrait of his wife held up by a small cupid. A river god sleeps behind the cupid and the earth goddess reclines in the background, while Aurora's winged horse waits under the trees. Poussin painted many mythological scenes in the 1630s for a group of scholarly connoisseurs who were interested in Ovid's writings. These pictures were also partly inspired by a revival of interest in sixteenth-century Venetian painting, and at that time a group of mythological paintings by Titian, including *Bacchus and Ariadne* (plate 18), were on view in Rome. Cephalus' pose is very close to that of Bacchus,

16. Nicolas Poussin (1594?–1665). Cephalus and Aurora

17. Piero di Cosimo (c. 1462– after 1515). A Mythological Subject

and the composition with the figures on a narrow stage in front of a screen of trees is also probably taken from Titian.

Another painting in the National Gallery (plate 17), by Piero di Cosimo, a Florentine artist working in the fifteenth and early sixteenth centuries, may illustrate the tragic finale. It depicts a woman lying dead, mourned by a satyr and a dog. The painting is sometimes called the *Death of Procris* but several details do not fit with the story as it is told in *Metamorphoses*. For example, Cephalus is not present, as he is in the poem, and the woman is wounded in the neck and wrists, and not, as Ovid describes, in the breast. It has been suggested that the artist used an intermediary source, identified as a play about Cephalus produced in Ferrara in 1487. The play, which was often performed at weddings as an admonition against jealousy, explains the presence of the satyr: it was he who set the seed of mistrust in Procris' mind by telling her about Zephyr.

Piero di Cosimo was renowned for his skill as an animal painter and for his mythological pictures, which show a detailed knowledge of classical texts and often strive to be accurate *all'antica* recreations of the stories. Although the shape of this painting might suggest it was originally set into a *cassone*, its excellent condition supports the theory that it was made as an independent painting, rather than as part of a piece of furniture.

BACCHUS AND ARIADNE

Ariadne was the daughter of the king of Crete. She saved the life of her lover, Theseus, by helping him escape from the labyrinth in which he had killed the Minotaur, a monster who was half-man and half-bull. The couple then set sail from Crete and came to the island of Naxos, where Theseus cruelly abandoned her. Ariadne wandered desolately on the sea shore until Bacchus, the god of wine, flew over the island on his way back from India and fell in love with her. Bacchus persuaded Ariadne to go away with him by promising to make her immortal:

> He took the crown from her forehead and set it as a constellation in the sky, to bring her eternal glory. Up through the thin air it soared and, as it flew, its jewels were changed into shining fires. They settled in position, still keeping the appearance of a crown, midway between the kneeling Hercules and Ophiuchus, who grasps the snake. (*Metamorphoses*, Book VIII, p. 184.)

Titian's painting (plate 18) depicts the moment of Bacchus' arrival, although the constellation, the Corona Borealis, is already visible in the sky above Ariadne. Theseus' departing boat can be seen on the horizon and Ariadne, who has been watching her lover sail away, turns round, startled, as Bacchus leaps from his chariot. He is accompanied by drunken revellers who clash noisy instruments and wave strange ritual objects; one wrestles with snakes tangled around his body and another clasps the severed limb of a cow.

The picture was commissioned by Alfonso d'Este, the ruler of Ferrara and a wealthy, cultivated patron of the arts. Alfonso already owned a mythological painting by Giovanni Bellini, the *Feast of the Gods* (now in the National Gallery in Washington), finished in 1514, and it seems that soon after this date he began planning a decorative scheme for his private study. The paintings were to illustrate descriptions of lost classical works of art, and were to be executed by the most famous artists of the day. Initially Alfonso commissioned Raphael and Fra Bartolommeo, but they died before completing their work.

After their deaths Titian gradually became more involved in the project, and finally painted three canvases for Alfonso, in addition to repainting parts of Bellini's picture to 'modernise' it. The two other paintings, *The Worship of Venus* and *The Andrians*, are now in the Prado in Madrid.

18. Titian (active before 1511, died 1576). Bacchus and Ariadne

The letter, quoted in the Introduction, from Titian to the Spanish king Philip II suggests that in the 1550s Titian enjoyed complete freedom in his interpretations of the Ovidian stories. However, when working for Alfonso d'Este he must have been given precise instructions, as *Bacchus and Ariadne* illustrates features from a number of texts in addition to *Metamorphoses*. For example, it is Philostratus (third century AD) who mentions that Bacchus' animals were cheetahs or leopards, and Ovid in another poem, the *Ars Amatoria (The Art of Love)*, who says that Bacchus leapt from his chariot. The actions of the wild revellers on the right are described in a poem by Catullus (first century BC) about the marriage of Peleus and Thetis. There was a coverlet on Peleus and Thetis' bed, and embroidered on it was the story of Ariadne, with Bacchus arriving followed by his drunken retinue.

Titian worked in Venice, which was then a rich port with trading links with the eastern Mediterranean. This gave him access to the best quality materials for making painters' pigments, especially lapis lazuli for making ultramarine blue. Vibrant contrasting colours can be seen throughout the painting – the blue sky, the red of Ariadne's spiralling sash, the yellow

cloak on the ground, the orange material on the cymbal-player. Titian set off the soft, sensual texture of flesh against bright draperies and gave each figure a pose that conveys a sense of energetic movement. These painterly devices evoke a dramatic and yet poignant image of the encounter between god and mortal.

THE STORY OF ORPHEUS

The poet Orpheus' power to move trees and animals with his music-making is illustrated in a painting by Roelandt Savery (plate 19). Orpheus, seated on the left, plays a stringed instrument (not the lyre specified by Ovid) to an audience of every conceivable type of bird, animal, plant and tree. Ovid describes how Orpheus' music was so harmonious that trees moved towards him to surround him with a shady grove.

Orpheus was grief-stricken as he played because he had failed to recover his wife, Eurydice, from the underworld. She had died from a snake-bite and although Orpheus had been granted permission to lead her back to earth, he had disobeyed his instructions and had looked round to see if she was following him. She then sank back, lost to him for ever. Thereafter Orpheus lost all interest in women, preferring young boys, and despite his music he was savagely killed by vengeful women, angry at his rejection of them.

This is one of several dozen versions of the subject painted by Savery. It is not the tragedy of Orpheus' story which concerned him, but the magic of the poet's music, which allowed him to paint landscapes with an encyclopedic range of botanical and zoological detail. The paintings reflect various aspects of the artist's unusual career. In 1605 he settled in Prague, working for the emperor, Rudolf II, and over the next few years he made many studies of the animals and birds in the emperor's famous zoo. He was also sent by the emperor to record the dramatic mountain scenery of the Tyrol and his paintings include alpine scenes.

By 1619 Savery was living in Utrecht, where he stayed until his death in 1639. This painting, dated 1628, is very much a fantasy, but despite its capriciousness it is based firmly on the artist's earlier observation of natural phenomena. It seems that in so using his studies from nature Savery contributed to the development of realistic landscape painting in the Netherlands in the first quarter of the seventeenth century.

19. Roelandt Savery (1576–1639). Orpheus

THE STORY OF MIDAS

King Midas was the victim of his own foolishness on two occasions. First, when offered a gift by Bacchus, he asked that everything he touched be turned to gold. This was granted, but his joy was short-lived as he discovered that food, too, came under the spell. Eventually Bacchus had to intervene to prevent Midas from starving to death.

On the second occasion, illustrated here by Domenichino (plate 20), the gods were less benevolent. Midas was asked to give his opinion at a musical competition between Apollo, seated on the right, and Pan, on the left. Apollo had played the lyre and Pan the reed pipes, and their performances had already been assessed by Tmolus, god of the mountain in the background. Tmolus knew Apollo was the superior musician but Midas disagreed and insisted that Pan was better. In punishment, Apollo – who was, after all, the god of music – gave Midas ass's ears as a sign of his foolish 'deafness'.

The painting is one of a series of ten frescoes which decorated the walls of

20. Dominichino (1581–1641) and Assistant(s). The Judgement of Midas

a summerhouse in the gardens of the Villa Aldobrandini at Frascati. The soft, pastel colours are characteristic of fresco painting, a technique in which colours are applied to wet plaster. The series depicts stories from Ovid about Apollo and each episode has a landscape setting – this example with the mountain, hill-town and waterfall is one of the finest. The landscapes were intended to harmonise with the pastoral setting of the villa, a rural retreat only a day's ride from metropolitan Rome. Resting or dining in the cool summerhouse, where a fountain played over a mock Mount Parnassus inhabited by sculptures of Apollo and the nine Muses, the landscapes enabled city-dwellers to imagine themselves in the eternal summer of Ovid's lost world.

Several of the frescoes show Apollo in vengeful mood – not only punishing Midas, but commanding the flaying of the satyr Marsyas who also dared to challenge his musical supremacy, killing two giant cyclops in revenge for the death of his son Aesculapius, and causing the death of the nymph Coronis who had been unfaithful to him. Some of these stories were rarely painted, which suggests that Domenichino was provided with a 'programme' by a learned adviser.

Domenichino was primarily a figure painter, but he also made an important contribution to the development of landscape painting, which was attracting increasing interest throughout Europe in the early seventeenth century. The Villa Aldobrandini series is innovative in the way in which the landscape dominates the figures but also offers a habitable space – we are persuaded that the gods, nymphs and satyrs could walk away into the depth of the painting. Despite this sense of realistic space and scale, the landscapes are idealised; in each scene the weather is tranquil and the light even, and the composition is an artificial arrangement of natural forms. This is the standard formula for classical landscape as developed by Claude in Rome later in the seventeenth century (see plates 7, 12 and 26).

THE LAPITHS AND THE CENTAURS

O vid describes several battles in brutal detail in *Metamorphoses*. A picture in the National Gallery (plate 21) by Piero di Cosimo, probably made as part of the wall-panelling, illustrates the long and bloody fight after the wedding of Pirithous, the Lapith king, and his bride, Hippodame. The centaurs, creatures who were half-man and half-horse, had been invited to the wedding. Unfortunately, centaurs were particularly prone to violent behaviour if they drank too much, and on this occasion Eurytus, one of the fiercest, was overcome with lust for the Lapith bride. He tried to rape her, and his companions began to assault the other Lapith women.

21. Piero di Cosimo (c. 1642– after 1515). The Fight between the Lapiths and the Centaurs

Several legendary heroes were at the feast, including Hercules and Theseus, and they helped to defend the Lapiths. Ovid describes many individual encounters, and parts of his text are illustrated faithfully in the painting. For example, in the group on the right we can see the centaur Eurytus grasping the bride's hair, while Theseus (the slayer of the Minotaur) hurls a decorated vessel at him – just as Ovid describes. Behind this group one centaur uses a candelabrum as a weapon, while another prepares to throw the smoking altar – both details are in the poem.

A poignant episode in the battle is illustrated in the centre foreground. A handsome male centaur, Cyllarus, has been fatally wounded in the fight by a huge spear. His lover Hylomene, whose hair has been combed and entwined with flowers, embraces him and tries to keep him alive. When she sees that he is dead she commits suicide.

According to Vasari, who wrote a biography of the artist in the mid-sixteenth century, Piero di Cosimo was somewhat eccentric. He disliked the noise of city life and preferred solitude; he lived on boiled eggs, which he cooked in advance in large quantities. Although he avoided human company, he loved to study animals and anything strange in the natural world. Evidence of the artist's observation of animal life can be seen in many of his paintings.

Some of Piero's work (for example, the *Forest Fire* in the Ashmolean Museum, Oxford) is about humanity in its primeval state, showing the early use of fire, the building of houses and the emergence of family life. The originality and wit of many details in Piero's works suggest that he was also familiar with a variety of classical sources. It may be that some of the grotesque behaviour in the *Lapiths and Centaurs* should be considered as mock heroic, especially in relation to more dignified paintings of the nude by contemporary artists such as Antonio Pollaiuolo and Luca Signorelli.

VENUS AND CUPID

The most frequently painted female mythological figure was Venus, goddess of love. Classical literature included numerous stories in which she played both a major and a minor role, and many of these were illustrated by artists. As the goddess of sexual desire, Venus could legitimately be painted naked, so if a patron required an image of a beautiful, nude woman he would commission a Venus.

Large-scale paintings of Venus began to appear in Italy at the end of the fifteenth century, and then spread throughout Europe. They are usually frankly erotic in intention despite their veneer of 'mythological' respectability. In these paintings Venus is often not taking part in any obvious narrative, but simply reclining on a bed or lying in a landscape (fig. 7). It seems that paintings of this type, which we now consider primarily as works of art and not as titillating erotica, were in some circles perceived as indecorous. During his visit to the Spanish court at Madrid in 1626, the Italian cleric and scholar, Cassiano dal Pozzo, recorded that mythological paintings containing nudes were covered in

Fig. 7 Giorgione (active 1506, died 1510) and Titian (active before 1511, died 1576). Sleeping Venus. *Dresden, Staatliche Gemäldegalerie*

Queen Isabella's presence.

Post-classical tradition accepted Cupid as Venus' child, although it is unclear who fathered him. Cupid is also a love god, whose attributes are wings, a bow and a quiver full of arrows. The arrows, often fired mischievously by Cupid, cause the pain and pleasure of sexual attraction. Sometimes Cupid was painted merely as an attribute of Venus, to identify her, but one late classical author, Apuleius (second century AD), tells the story of Cupid's own love affair with Psyche, a story which is illustrated in two National Gallery paintings.

THE SCHOOL OF LOVE

According to Renaissance humanists, Venus symbolised the different types of love. For example, she could represent intellectual love, controlling and promoting harmony, as seems to be the case here (plate 22), where Cupid is being taught to read by Mercury. In a painting by Correggio in the Louvre (fig. 8) – probably the pendant to the National Gallery canvas – Venus is shown asleep in an immodest pose spied on by a lustful satyr; there she probably represents sensual love and uncontrolled carnal passion.

It is unusual in Italian art for Venus to be shown winged, as she is in the National Gallery painting. In northern Italy in the fifteenth century, however, she did sometimes have wings when she represented a planetary goddess. In this painting Correggio may be referring to medieval astrological tradition: as personifications of the planets named after them, Mercury and Venus may be passing on their benevolent influences of reason and humanity to Cupid. This is not to imply that the '*School of Love*' is not intended as a celebration of the female nude, but there is also a strong element of charming domesticity about the image, perhaps suggesting it was commissioned to celebrate the birth of a child.

The '*School of Love*' is one of only six easel paintings with mythological subjects executed by Correggio, a contemporary of Raphael, who worked mainly in Parma in northern Italy. The mythologies were probably all commissioned by Federigo Gonzaga, Duke of Mantua, to decorate a villa designed for relaxation and pleasure. The other paintings include illustrations of Jupiter's love affairs with Danaë, Leda, Ganymede and Io.

The National Gallery painting seems to date from the mid-1520s and

22. Correggio (active 1514, died 1534). Mercury instructing Cupid before Venus ('The School of Love')

X-radiographs reveal that Correggio made major changes as he evolved the composition. At one stage Venus was seated where Mercury now appears; then, when she was first painted standing in her present position, she looked down towards Mercury and Cupid, closing the group. The final version is rather more titillating — Venus invites the viewer's gaze.

Such major changes, and the way in which the figures are modelled, suggest that Correggio was aware of Venetian painting techniques as they developed during the first quarter of the sixteenth century. Venetian artists such as Giorgione and Titian tended to exploit the effects of blending and layering oil paint. Although for some projects Correggio did many preparatory drawings, as would be usual for Florentine or Roman artists, in this painting he has developed the composition directly on the canvas in the

Fig. 8 Correggio (active 1514, died 1534). Venus and a Satyr. *Paris, Louvre*

Venetian manner. The volume of the figures is built up in layers of colour with a disregard for accurate anatomy, and large areas of shadow soften and disguise the contours. By contrast, some textures – especially hair and feathers – are painted in considerable detail. The final effect is a perfect expression of the sensuality and tenderness of the subject.

VENUS AND MARS

One of Venus' lovers was Mars, god of war, but her husband, Vulcan, eventually discovered his wife's infidelity and trapped the couple in a magic invisible net. Botticelli's panel (plate 23) is concerned only with Venus and Mars as lovers and makes no reference to their exposure. Mars is unarmed and exhausted after love-making; Venus is coolly aloof and more dominant, maintaining her dignity because she is clothed. The implicit meaning of the painting is that love can conquer war.

The shape of the panel suggests that it was originally either part of a piece of furniture, perhaps a bed or a seat, or part of decorative room-panelling. E. H. Gombrich has hypothesised that the wasps which swarm noisily by Mars' head are a punning reference to the coat of arms of the Vespucci family, in which there is a band of wasps – *vespa* is the Italian for wasp. Perhaps, since the subject-matter would be appropriate for the decoration of a nuptial chamber, the panel was commissioned by the Vespucci family to celebrate a wedding.

The Vespucci belonged to a small group of Florentine connoisseurs who commissioned from Botticelli mythological paintings with complex mean- ings. These patrons' interest in the classical past was strongly influenced by contemporary Neo-Platonic philosophy, in which pagan myths were seen as allegories which, when decoded, revealed Christian truths. For example, the story of the mortal Psyche's love for Cupid (see plates 25 and 26) was believed to show the longing of the mortal soul for divine beauty and truth.

Marsilio Ficino was one of the most influential Neo-Platonic philo- sophers in Florence and it is likely that the unusual contrast between the two figures, with Venus dominant and Mars relaxed and somnolent, reflects Ficino's astrological interpretation of the myth:

> Mars is outstanding in strength among the planets because he makes men stronger, but Venus masters him . . . Venus, when in conjunction

23. Sandro Botticelli (c. *1445–1510).* Venus and Mars

with Mars, in opposition to him, or in reception . . . seems to master and appease Mars, but Mars never masters Venus. (Quoted by E. H. Gombrich in *Symbolic Images*, London 1972, p. 67).

In addition there is probably an allusion to a lost classical painting. Lucian, a writer of the second century AD, describes a painting of the marriage of Alexander and Roxana in which cupids played with Alexander's spear and armour. The little satyrs here seem to illustrate the description.

Botticelli shared many of the preoccupations of early Renaissance artists: Mars' torso has probably been studied from life, and the entire painting is, of course, a sophisticated celebration of antiquity. However, he was not totally committed to the Renaissance theory of naturalism, proposed by Alberti, which held that a painting should be the mirror of reality, creating in particular the illusion of a third dimension. The composition of *Venus and Mars* is clearly two-dimensional and the proportions of the two main figures are unconvincing – Venus' shoulders and right leg hardly exist, while Mars' legs are too short to support his body. The strength and beauty of the composition lie not in its naturalism but in the sense of line and the pattern of gestures and shapes repeated across the surface.

CUPID COMPLAINING TO VENUS

Lucas Cranach's painting (plate 24) is primarily a display of the female body, but there is a minor narrative element: Cupid, who holds a honeycomb, is complaining to his mother that he is being stung by bees. The theme is explained in the top right-hand corner by a Latin verse loosely based on a Greek poem, 'The Honeycomb Stealer', written in the third century BC by Theocritus.

Venus, displaying herself to the viewer, epitomises sensuality, and her promise of lascivious pleasure is reinforced by the traditional symbols of female sexuality, the apple and honey. The stag behind the tree provides a suggestive male presence. The apple tree and the lush vegetation possibly allude to Eve in the Garden of Eden, so the woman is both Venus and Eve, picking the apple of humanity's downfall.

Despite her mythological persona, Venus maintains a vestige of contemporaneity – which presumably made her more alluring to a sixteenth-century male viewer – for she wears a courtly, feathered hat and heavy necklaces. The implication is that a 'modern' woman has undressed to play the role of Venus.

The painting was probably completed around 1530 in Wittenberg, where Cranach worked at the court of the Elector of Saxony. (Cranach's monogram, a winged snake, is clearly visible on the large stone by Venus' feet.) In 1528 Philipp Melanchthon, Professor of Greek at Wittenberg University, translated Theocritus' poem into Latin. Cranach almost certainly knew Melanchthon, and the painting was probably for a member of the sophisticated circle of Wittenberg humanists. Although Albrecht Dürer, Cranach's more famous contemporary, had made a drawing of the same subject in 1514, Cranach is the first German artist to produce numerous independent panel paintings of mythological subjects. He painted several Venuses, with and without Cupid, and at least a dozen versions of the Judgement of Paris. Here, the slim hips and high waist of the goddess, silhouetted against dark foliage, represent a Northern European type of idealised female beauty very different from the fuller-figured Italian Venus, who is based on ancient Roman sculptures.

24. Lucas Cranach the Elder (1472–1553). Cupid complaining to Venus

PSYCHE AND CUPID

The story of Cupid and Psyche is told within the main narrative of Lucius Apuleius' book *Metamorphoses*, popularly known as *The Golden Ass*. Apuleius was born in the Roman province of Morocco, and his book, written in the second century AD, describes his conversion to the religious cult of the goddess Isis, although to a modern reader it seems to be simply a collection of entertaining and racy stories. Jean-Honoré Fragonard, whose painting (plate 25) depicts the first part of the story, probably knew the Psyche legend from a seventeenth-century version by La Fontaine, *Les Amours de Psyché et de Cupidon*.

Psyche was a princess, and so beautiful that her father's subjects abandoned the shrines of Venus to worship her instead. Angry and jealous, Venus sent her son Cupid to make Psyche fall in love with a thoroughly worthless man. But the unforeseen happened: Cupid himself fell in love with Psyche.

Psyche was introduced to Cupid in strange circumstances. Her parents were told by Apollo's oracle to lead their daughter in her wedding dress to a remote mountain-top, where they were to leave her. They obeyed the instructions and returned home. Then, unknown to them, Psyche was carried magically by the wind into the grounds of a magnificent building, clearly the residence of an immortal. Inside the palace Psyche saw no one, but was guided by sweet voices. She found fine clothes and jewellery, exquisite food and fragrant water to bathe in. At night Cupid came to her bed and made love to her, but he always departed before daylight and Psyche remained ignorant of his identity. All went well, until Psyche persuaded her lover to let her see her sisters again. She brought them back to the palace and showed them her new possessions. In their jealousy, the sisters plotted to destroy Psyche's miraculous good fortune.

It is this moment which Fragonard has illustrated. Psyche reclines on the right, innocent of the effect the display is having on her sisters standing in the centre. Above them, Eris, goddess of discord, represents the distress the sisters will cause. Fragonard has seen the story as an opportunity to paint a group of elegantly idealised and scantily clad women adorned with fabrics and flowers. This sensual feast is rendered with great virtuosity by the delicate, transparent layers of paint, and the choice of warm, contrasting colours.

The painting is a brilliant example of French Rococo, a style whose fashionable appeal was partly due to the taste and patronage of Madame de

25. Jean-Honoré Fragonard (1732–1806). Psyche showing her Sisters her Gifts from Cupid

Pompadour and Louis XV. It is thought that the picture was shown at Versailles and admired by the king and Madame de Pompadour. Fragonard's teacher, François Boucher, worked at court and frequently designed decorative cycles of mythologies; this composition is based on a tapestry design of the same subject by Boucher.

As Fragonard indicates, Psyche's happiness was now threatened. Her sisters persuaded her to identify her mysterious lover. They frightened her: maybe he would turn into a deadly snake and devour her. On their advice, one night Psyche sharpened a knife, ready to kill her lover, and hid it with a lamp in her bedroom. When Cupid fell asleep Psyche saw for the first time that he was the god of love himself. She fell on him with renewed passion, but spilt oil from the lamp on his shoulder. Cupid took one look at the lamp and the knife, and flew out of the window up into the sky with Psyche clinging in desperation to his leg. The poor girl soon grew tired and fell to earth, unharmed, but quite alone.

A painting in the National Gallery by Claude (plate 26) presumably shows Psyche's exile from Cupid's palace, although the artist himself appears to have given it no title. It has become known as '*The Enchanted Castle*', the title given to an engraving of the painting published in England in 1782. It is one of the artist's finest late works, painted in 1664 for Prince Lorenzo Colonna. The prince commissioned at least nine paintings from Claude in the last twenty years of the artist's life; they often have rare subjects from classical literature, as is the case here, and sometimes include motifs of personal significance to the patron.

The composition of *Psyche outside the Palace of Cupid* is a variation on Claude's earlier seaport paintings (three of which can be seen in the National Gallery), with their fanciful harbours, elaborate buildings and

26. Claude (1600–1682). Landscape with Psyche outside the Palace of Cupid ('The Enchanted Castle')

ornate but unsailable ships. The light from the rising or setting sun reflected in the water and playing over the architecture was probably the most admired feature of the paintings. Sometimes the seaport scenes had a specific narrative subject, which was usually the embarkation or disembarkation of a biblical figure. In the earlier ones the figures and the story, such as it is, can seem extraneous, but in '*The Enchanted Castle*' every part of the painting – the distant palace, the rocky outcrops on the left, the endless expanse of sea, the cold light – contributes to the impression of Psyche's total isolation.

But what of Cupid and Psyche? The lovers were eventually reunited, despite Venus' attempt to kill Psyche by setting her impossible tasks, including a visit to the underworld. It was Jupiter who decreed that Psyche should become an immortal, and that Cupid would be kept out of mischief by marrying her. The wedding was celebrated by all the gods and goddesses at a great feast:

> Presently a great wedding breakfast was prepared. Cupid reclined in the place of honour with Psyche's head resting on his breast; Jupiter was placed next, with Juno in the same comfortable postion, and then all the other gods and goddesses in order of seniority. Jupiter was served with nectar and ambrosia by apple-cheeked Ganymede, his personal cup-bearer; Bacchus attended to everyone else. Vulcan was the chef; the Hours decorated the palace with red roses and other bridal flowers; the Graces sprinkled balsam water; the Muses chanted the marriage-hymn to the accompaniment of flute and pipe-music from the godlings Satyrus and Peniscus. Finally Apollo sang to his own lyre and the music was so sweet that Venus came forward and performed a lively step-dance in time to it. Psyche was properly married to Cupid and in due time she bore him her child, a daughter whose name was Pleasure. (Apuleius, *The Golden Ass*, p. 133.)

LIST OF PLATES

The dimensions are in centimeters followed by inches. Height is followed by width.

1. Joachim Wtewael, *The Judgement of Paris*. 1615. Wood, 54.7 × 74.1 (23½ × 31⅛). London, National Gallery

2. Peter Paul Rubens, *The Judgement of Paris*. Probably around 1632–5. Wood, 144.8 × 193.7 (57 × 76¼). London, National Gallery

3. Follower of Fra Angelico, *The Abduction of Helen*. Probably around 1450. Wood, 50.8 × 61 (20 × 24). London, National Gallery

4. Giovanni Domenico Tiepolo, *The Building of the Trojan Horse*. 1750s. Canvas, 38.8 × 66.7 (15¼ × 26¼). London, National Gallery

5. Giovanni Domenico Tiepolo. *The Procession of the Trojan Horse into Troy*. 1750s. Canvas, 38.8 × 66.7 (15¼ × 26¼). London, National Gallery

6. Joseph Mallord William Turner, *Ulysses deriding Polyphemus*. Exhibited 1829. Canvas, 132.7 × 203.2 (52¼ × 80). London, National Gallery

7. Claude, *Landscape with Aeneas at Delos*. 1672. Canvas, approx. 99.7 × 134 (39¼ × 52¾). London, National Gallery

8. Ascribed to Antonio del Pollaiuolo, *Apollo and Daphne*. Probably 1460s. Wood, 29.5 × 20 (11⅜ × 7⅞). London, National Gallery

9. Pieter Lastman, *Juno discovering Jupiter with Io*. 1618. Wood, 54.3 × 77.8 (21⅜ × 30⅝). London, National Gallery

10. Cornelis van Haarlem, *Two Followers of Cadmus devoured by a Dragon*. 1588. Canvas, 148.5 × 195.5 (58½ × 77). London, National Gallery

11. Titian, *The Death of Actaeon*. 1560s. Canvas, 178.4 × 198.1 (70¼ × 78). London, National Gallery

12. Claude, *Landscape with Narcissus and Echo*. 1644. Canvas, 94.6 × 118.1 (37¼ × 46½). London, National Gallery

13. Follower of Giovanni Antonio Boltraffio, *Narcissus*. Probably around 1510. Wood, 23.2 × 26.4 (9⅛ × 10⅜). London, National Gallery

14. Luca Giordano, *Perseus turning Phineas and his Followers to Stone*. Around 1680. Canvas, 285 × 366 (168½ × 172). London, National Gallery

15. Peter Paul Rubens, *Aurora abducting Cephalus*. About 1636–7. Wood, approx. 30.8 × 48 (12⅛ × 19). London, National Gallery

16. Nicolas Poussin, *Cephalus and Aurora*. Late 1620s. Canvas, 96.5 × 130.8 (38 × 51½). London, National Gallery

17. Piero di Cosimo, *A Mythological Subject*. Around 1500. Wood, 65.4 × 184.2 (23¾ × 72¼). London, National Gallery

18. Titian, *Bacchus and Ariadne*. 1522–3. Canvas, 175.2 × 190.5 (69 × 75). London, National Gallery

19. Roelandt Savery, *Orpheus*. 1628. Wood, 53 × 81.5 (20⅞ × 32⅛). London, National Gallery

20. Domenichino and Assistant(s), *The Judgement of Midas*. Around 1616–18. Fresco, transferred to canvas, mounted on board, 267 × 224 (105¼ × 80¾). London, National Gallery

21. Piero di Cosimo, *The Fight between the Lapiths and the Centaurs*. Around 1500. Wood, 71 × 260 (28 × 102½). London, National Gallery

22. Correggio, *Mercury instructing Cupid before Venus ('The School of Love')*. Probably mid-1520s. Canvas, 155.6 × 91.4 (61¼ × 36). London, National Gallery

23. Sandro Botticelli, *Venus and Mars*. Probably 1480s. Wood, 69.2 × 173.4 (27¼ × 68¼). London, National Gallery

24. Lucas Cranach the Elder, *Cupid complaining to Venus*. Probably around 1530. Wood, 81.3 × 54.6 (32 × 21½). London, National Gallery

25. Jean-Honoré Fragonard, *Psyche showing her Sisters her Gifts from Cupid*. 1753. Canvas, 168.3 × 192.4 (66¼ × 75¾). London, National Gallery.

26. Claude, *Landscape with Psyche outside the Palace of Cupid ('The Enchanted Castle')*. 1664. Canvas, 87 × 151 (34¼ × 59½). London, National Gallery

FIGURES

Fig. 1 Fifteenth-century Florentine school, Cassone with a Tournament Scene. Carved and gilded wood, main panel 38.1 × 130.2 (15 × 51¼). London, National Gallery

Fig. 2 Albrecht Dürer, *Apollo and Diana*. Around 1502. Engraving, 115 × 70 (45¼ × 27½). London, British Museum

Fig. 3 Titian, *Danaë with Nursemaid*. 1553–4. Canvas, 129 × 180 (50¾ × 70¾). Madrid, Prado

Fig. 4 Giovanni Battista Tiepolo, *An Allegory with Venus and Time*. Before 1758. Canvas, 292 × 190.4 (115 × 75). London, National Gallery

Fig. 5 Ferdinand-Victor-Eugène Delacroix, *Ovid among the Scythians*. 1859. Canvas, 87.6 × 130.2 (34½ × 51¼). London, National Gallery

Fig. 6 Pablo Picasso, *Centaur, Bacchant and Faun*. 1947. Lithograph, 48.9 × 64.1 (19¼ × 25¼). London, Victoria and Albert Museum. © DACS 1988.

Fig. 7 Giorgione and Titian, *Sleeping Venus*. Around 1510–11. Canvas, 108.5 × 175 (42¾ × 68). Dresden, Gemäldegalerie

Fig. 8. Correggio, *Venus and Satyr*. Probably mild-1520s. Canvas, 188.5 × 125.5 (74¼ × 49½). Paris, Louvre

REFERENCES · THE STORIES

The stories can be found in: Apuleius, *The Golden Ass*; Homer, *The Odyssey*; Ovid, *Metamorphoses*; and Virgil, *The Aeneid*. All these works are available in the Loeb Classical Library, which gives both the original text and the English translation, and in the Penguin Classics series. For full references see under Further Reading. The page numbers given below refer to the Penguin editions.

THE TROJAN WAR
The Fall of Troy is described in *The Aeneid*, Book II. For the Procession of the Trojan Horse into Troy see Book II, pp. 41–2. For Odysseus's part see *The Odyssey*, Book IV, pp. 70–2, and Book VIII, pp. 135–6. The story of the Cyclops can be found in Book IX, pp. 142–54; for Turner's painting, *Ulysses deriding Polyphemus*, see pp. 152–3. For Claude's *Landscape with Aeneas at Delos* see *The Aeneid*, Book III, p. 68, and *Metamorphoses*, Book XIII, p. 302.

OVID'S 'METAMORPHOSES'
Book I: Apollo and Daphne, pp. 41–4; Jupiter and Io, pp. 44–9; Book III: Cadmus, pp. 74–7; Actaeon, pp. 77–80; Narcissus and Echo, pp. 83–7; Book IV: Perseus and Andromeda, pp. 112–15, and Book V, pp. 116–22; Book VII: The Story of Cephalus, pp. 174–8; Book VIII: Bacchus and Ariadne, pp. 183–4; Book X: Orpheus, pp. 225–7; Book XI: Orpheus, pp. 246–7; Midas, pp. 248–51; Book XII: The Lapiths and the Centaurs, pp. 273–82. [The quotations in the text are taken from *The Metamorphosis of Ovid*, trs. by Mary M. Innes, Penguin Classics, 1955. © Mary M. Innes 1955.]

VENUS AND CUPID
For the story of Venus and Mars see *Metamorphoses*, Book IV, pp. 98–9. The story of Cupid and Psyche can be found in *The Golden Ass* by Apuleius, Chapters VII–IX. [The quotation in the text is from *Apuleius's The Golden Ass*, trs. by Robert Graves, Penguin Classics, 1955. © Robert Graves. With the kind permission of A. P. Watt Ltd on behalf of the Executors of the Estate of Robert Graves.]

FURTHER READING

Apuleius, *The Golden Ass* (trs. by W. Adlington; revised by S. Gaselee), Loeb Classical Library, London 1912

Apuleius's The Golden Ass (trs. by Robert Graves), Penguin Classics, 1955

E. H. Gombrich, *Symbolic Images*, London 1972

R. Graves, *The Greek Myths*, 2 vols, revised edition, Harmondsworth 1960

J. Hall, *Dictionary of Subjects and Symbols in Art*, revised edition, London 1979

Homer, *The Odyssey* (trs. by A. T. Murray), Loeb Classical Library, London 1919

Homer, *The Odyssey* (trs. by E. V. Rieu), Penguin Classics, 1946 reprinted 1986

Ovid, *Metamorphoses* (trs. by F. J. Miller), Loeb Classical Library, London 1916

Ovid, *Metamorphoses* (trs. by M. M. Innes), Penguin Classics, 1955

Erwin Panofsky, *Renaissance and Renaissances in Western Art*, Princeton N.J. 1965

B. Radice, *Who's Who in the Ancient World: A Handbook to the Survivors of the Greek and Roman Classics*, revised edition, Harmondsworth 1973

J. Seznec, *The Survival of the Pagan Gods*, New York 1953

Virgil (trs. by H. R. Fairclough), 2 vols, Loeb Classical Library, London 1912

Virgil, *The Aeneid* (trs. by R. Fitzgerald), King Penguin, 1983

INDEX

Numbers in *italic* refer to the illustrations